INGO ARNDT

Best Foot Forward

Exploring Feet, Flippers, and Claws

Translated by J. Alison James

Holiday House / New York

Whose foot is this?

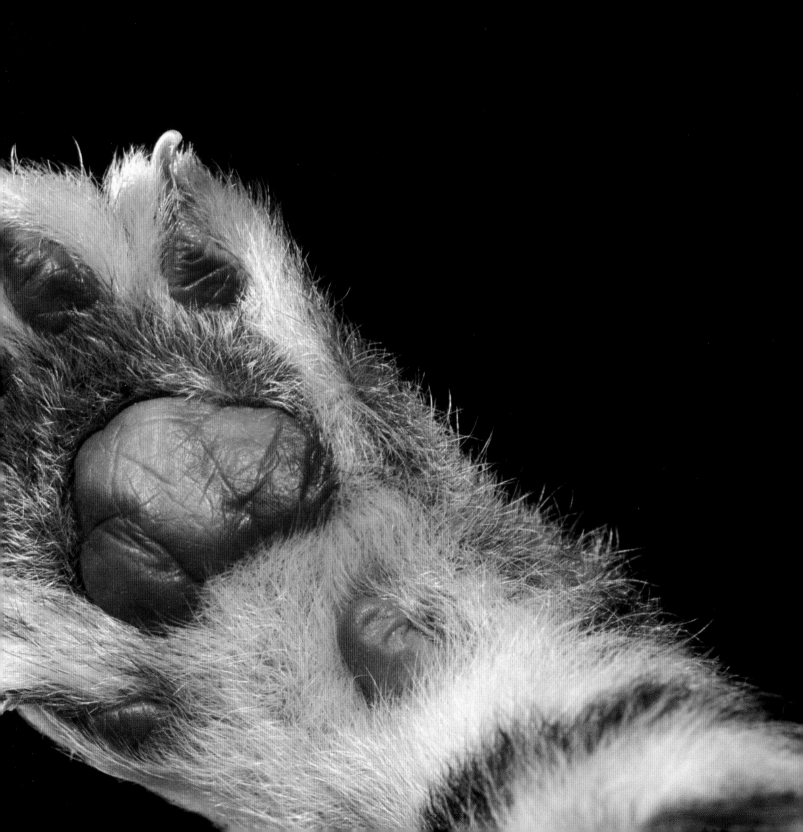

A tiger's.

With the soft, cushioned pads on its feet, a tiger can creep up very quietly on its prey and then—*click*—out come the claws!

Animals have very different feet depending on whether they are big or small, go fast or slow, or travel on the ground, in water, or high in the tops of trees.

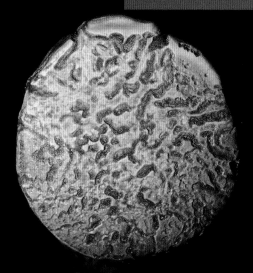

This is the foot of a copse snail. Its wave-like motions enable the snail to crawl across a meadow.

This is the giant foot of an elephant. Since an elephant is so big and heavy, the soles of its feet are soft and springy to help cushion its walk.

With this foot, the long-horned beetle can climb tree trunks and branches. The hairs on the underside of the foot keep it from slipping off.

An ostrich has only two toes, but these toes grip and help the bird run remarkably fast.

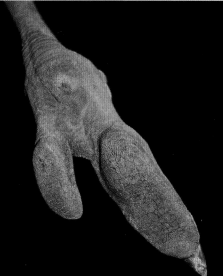

Whose foot is this?

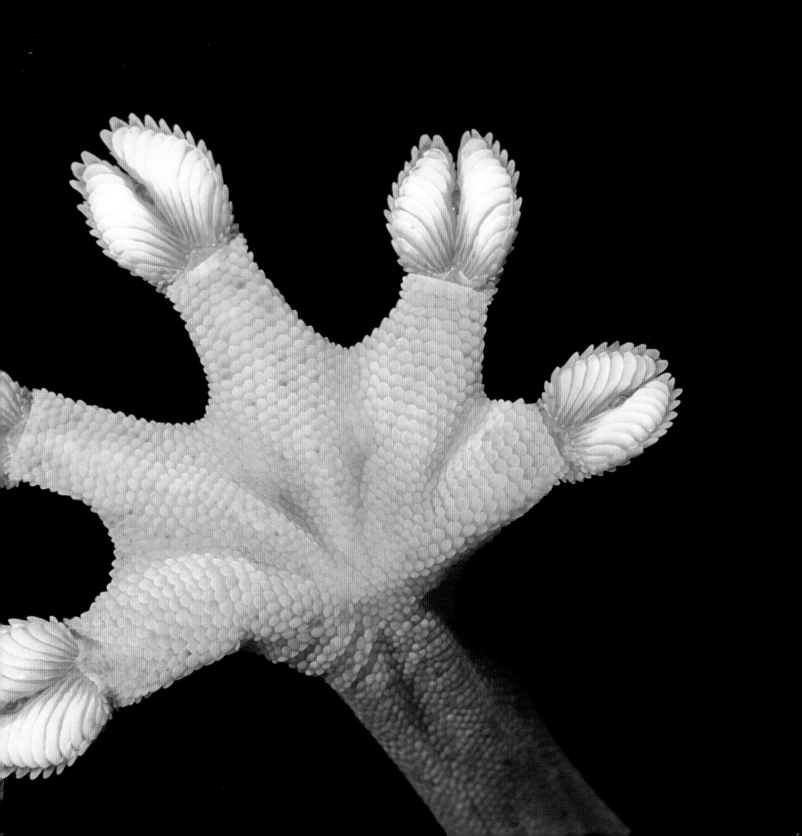

A leaf-tailed gecko's.

The gecko hunts for insects high up in the trees.

Animals that live in trees need feet for walking and for climbing.

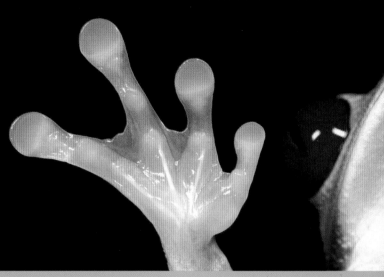

The red-eyed tree frog climbs the trees of the rain forest. It uses its toes to grip onto branches and even onto leaves.

A sticky liquid comes out of the toes of the red-eyed tree frog that helps the frog hold on tight.

Another gecko, the tokay, has ribbed toes that cling to smooth surfaces so it can climb up walls and walk along the ceiling.

The chimpanzee can grip with its feet, which help it swing through the trees.

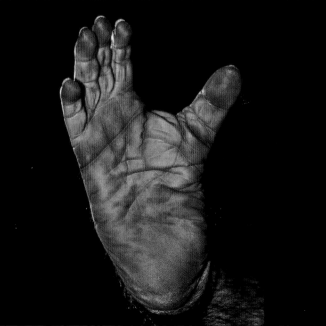

Whose foot is this?

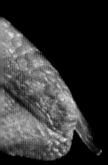

A duck's.

The webbing between its toes makes the duck an expert at paddling.

Animals that swim need feet that help propel them in water.

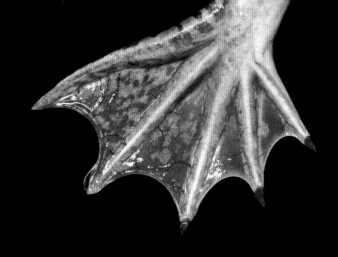

This is the back foot of the Australian freshwater crocodile. The webbing helps the crocodile climb up slippery, muddy riverbanks.

The African clawed frog also has powerful webbed feet on its back legs.

This is the foot of a seal. It's called a flipper.

Seals can't walk at all—they wriggle on their stomachs and use their flippers for swimming.

Whose foot is this?

A tortoise's.

The tortoise uses its strong claws to dig in the sand.

Animals don't just use their feet to walk, climb, or swim. Some use them for digging.

The mole's feet are like strong shovels with long, flat claws. They are perfect feet for digging long tunnels under the ground.

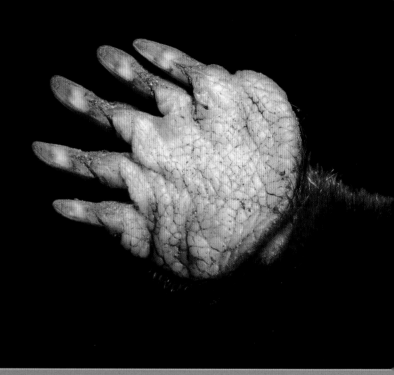

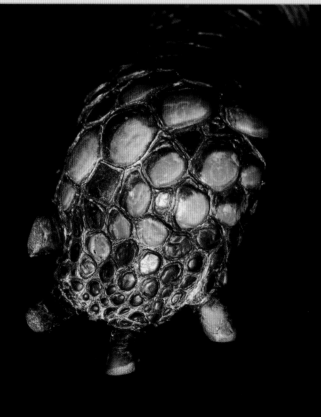

This beautiful spotted foot belongs to the red-footed tortoise, which lives in the Amazon rain forest in South America. A female digs a nest for her eggs deep in the moist soil.

Whose foot is this?

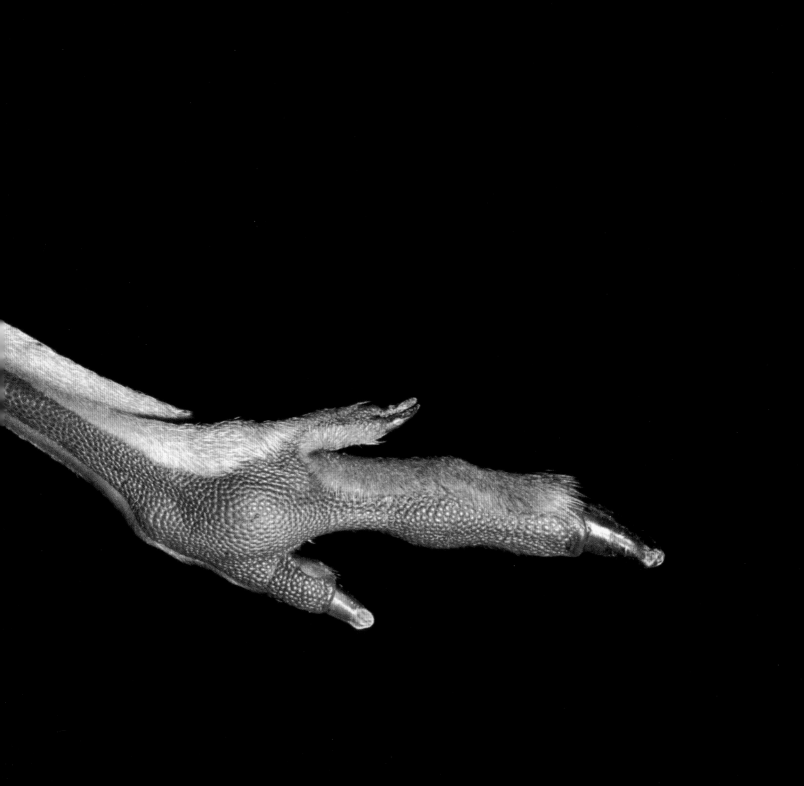

A kangaroo's.

With its very long back feet, the kangaroo can jump as far as 12 meters (40 feet).

Animals that depend on jumping need powerful legs and strong feet.

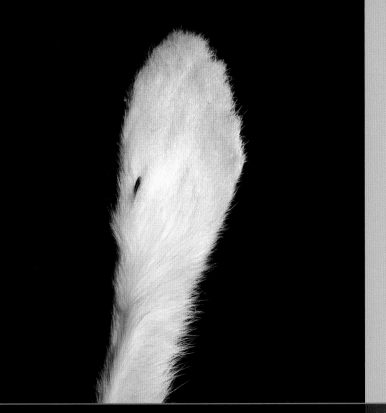

The snow hare also can jump fast and far. The thick fur on its feet keep it from sinking into the soft snow.

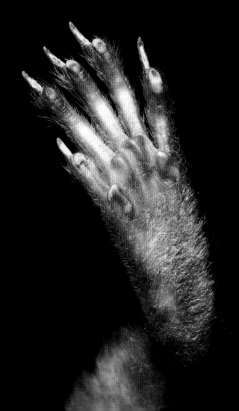

With its clingy toes, the squirrel is a very skillful climber. Strong back legs and feet help it spring from tree to tree.

Whose foot is this?

A lobster's.

The lobster has feet like snapping scissors on six of its ten legs.

Feet can be quite extraordinary.

The sea star has five arms with hundreds of tiny suction feet that help it grip the ocean floor and not be swept away in the current.

An octopus also has suction cups on its eight tentacles.

Short, stubby legs help this death's-head hawkmoth caterpillar climb up plants to find good leaves to eat.

The caterpillar's feet have moist bristles that help keep it from falling off.

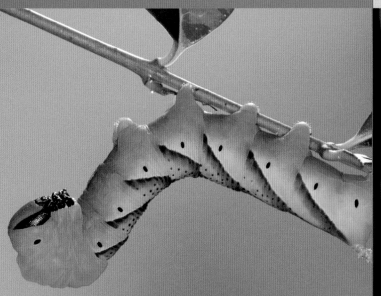

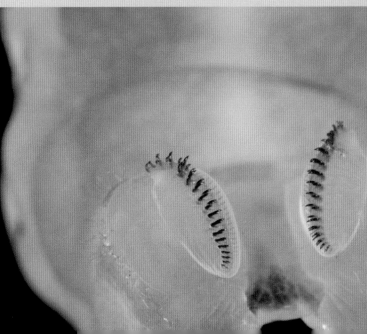

Index of Animals

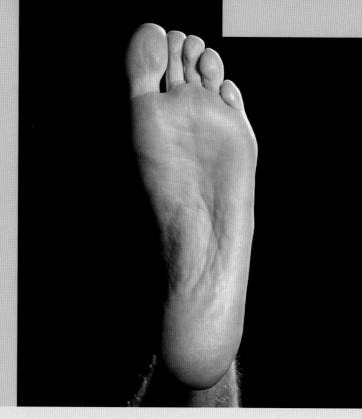

Whose foot is this?
Ingo Arndt's. Ingo is the author of
this book and took all the pictures
of the animal feet.

Ingo Arndt was born in Frankfurt am Main, Germany. He has worked as a
wildlife photographer since 1992 and uses his photographs to advocate for
nature conservation. He travels the world with his camera, to places such
as the Amazon, the Arctic, and Africa. His photos can also be seen in *GEO*
magazine and on his website: www.ingoarndt.com.

First published in Germany in 2007 by Patmos Verlag GmbH,
Sauerländer Verlag, Düsseldorf.
Text and illustrations copyright © 2007 by Bibliographisches
Institut GmbH, successor in interest of Patmos Verlag GmbH,
Sauerländer Verlag.
First published in the United States of America in 2013
by Holiday House, Inc.
Translation copyright © 2013 by Holiday House, Inc.
Translated by J. Alison James
All Rights Reserved
HOLIDAY HOUSE is registered in the U.S. Patent
and Trademark Office.
Printed and Bound in April 2013 at Toppan Leefung,
DonGuan City, China.
www.holidayhouse.com
First U.S. Edition
1 3 5 7 9 10 8 6 4 2

Library of Congress Cataloging-in-Publication Data
Arndt, Ingo, 1968-
[Zeigt her eure F|sse. English]
Best foot forward : exploring feet, flippers, and claws /
by Ingo Arndt. — First American edition.
pages cm
Audience: Ages 4-8.
Audience: Grades K to grade 3.
ISBN 978-0-8234-2857-1 (hardcover)
1. Foot—Juvenile literature. I. Title.
QL950.7.A76 2013
591.47—dc23
 2012039295